THE SEED

by Kazuko Nakazawa

Illustrated by Osamu Tsurata and Gilberto Corretti

EARLY BIRD COLLECTION AUTHORS

John McInnes, *Senior Author*   Glen Dixon   John Ryckman

I am a small seed.
My name is "bean"
and I belong to vegetable life.
I want to tell you my story.
Winter is over,
and the ants are back at work.
The earth will be my new home.
Someone has dug a hole
and planted me in it.

It is very dark and quiet in the earth.
I feed from my seed leaves.
Soon my coat splits open
and I grow a small root.

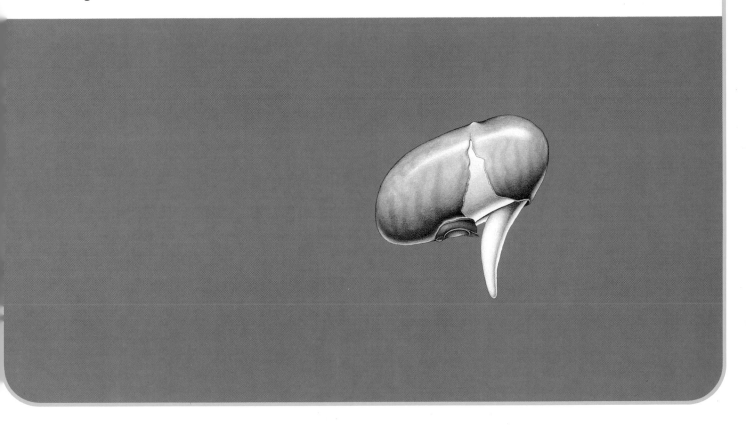

My root grows quickly.
It pushes me steadily up
towards the sun
above the earth.
My skin has burst open
because I have grown too big for it.

Look, I have germinated!
I am out in the fresh air
and sunlight.
Life feels good.
My seed leaves are full
of good nourishment.
The little ant looks up at me.
He can hardly believe his eyes.

Look at my leaves,
wet with morning dew.
Feel them—they are covered
with a layer of fine hairs.
My stalk and roots help to feed me
so that I can grow and grow.

I like to grow
round and round something.
It helps to keep me up
now that I'm bigger.
I am growing new leaves
all the while—and three at a time!

Now my flowers
are ready to open.
They are all yellow.
The butterflies
like to fly
around them.

My yellow flowers fall off, and in their place I grow a green pod.
Inside the pod, buds of future beans will grow
and these will be protected by a fine shell.

See how many pods I've grown.
You can see the shapes
of the little beans inside.
Look, there's
a green grasshopper
on one of my pods!
I didn't notice him
at first! Did you?

Now I'm feeling rather old.
All this growing
has made me tired.
All my leaves
are turning brown.

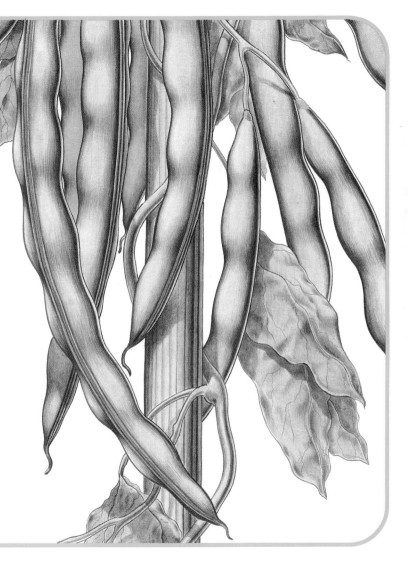

A dragonfly is interested
in one of my pods.
Perhaps he knows
the little beans are ready...

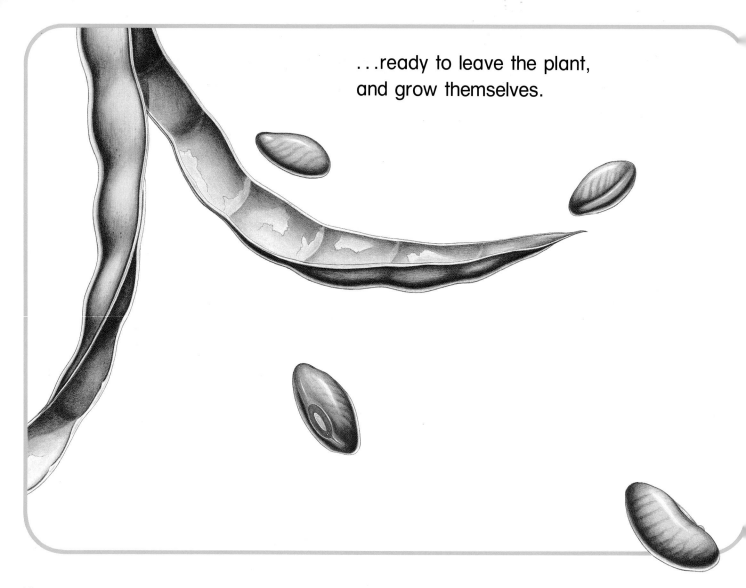

...ready to leave the plant,
and grow themselves.

See how many little beans there are—brown, smooth, and shiny!
And can you remember?—we only started off with me!
The big hands can't hold them all.

Some will fall back to earth
and drop into those little holes
for planting.
And now you know...
my story is just the same
for every one of those beans!

PUBLISHED SIMULTANEOUSLY IN 1990 BY:

Nelson Canada,
A Division of Thomson
Canada Limited
1120 Birchmount Road
Scarborough, Ontario   M1K 5G4

AND

Delmar Publishers Inc.,
A Division of Thomson Corp.
2 Computer Drive, West
Box 15015
Albany, NY 12212-5015

**Canadian Cataloguing
in Publication Data**

Nakazawa, Kazuko
   The seed

(Early bird collection)
ISBN 0-17-603115-4

1. Seeds - Juvenile literature.   I. Tsurata, Osamu.
II. Corretti, Gilbert.   III. Title.   IV. Series.

QK661.N35 1990   j582'.0467   C90-093205-8

**Library of Congress
Cataloging-in-Publication Data**

Nakazawa, Kazuko
   [Tane, English]
   The seed/by Kazuko Nakazawa; illustrations by Osamu
Tsurata and Gilberto Corretti.

   p. cm.—(Early bird)
   Translation of: Tane.
   Summary: A bean recounts its life story, from under-
ground seed to flowering plant to producer of new beans.
   ISBN 0-8273-4117-2
   1. Plants - Juvenile literature.   2. Plant life cycles -
Juvenile literature. 3. Seeds - Juvenile literature.
[1. Plants.   2. Plant life cycles.   3. Seeds.]
I. Tsurata, Osamu, ill.   II. Corretti, Gilberto, ill.
III. Title.   IV. Series: Early bird (Albany, N.Y.)
QK49.N2813 1989   581—dc20   89-27550
                                               CIP
                                               AC

Reprinted by permission of frobel-kan company limited.

Co-ordinating Editor: Jean Stinson
Project Managers: Jocelyn Van Huyse-Wilson/Norma Kennedy
Editors: Irene Cox/Lisa Collins
Art Director: Lorraine Tuson
Series Design and Art Direction: Rob McPhail
Typesetting: Nelson Canada
1234567890 EB 9876543210